Jul 2020

COMANCHE

Big Buddy Books

An Imprint of Abdo Publishing
abdopublishing.com

abdopublishing.com

Published by Abdo Publishing, a division of ABDO, PO Box 398166, Minneapolis, Minnesota 55439.
Copyright © 2019 by Abdo Consulting Group, Inc. International copyrights reserved in all countries. No part
of this book may be reproduced in any form without written permission from the publisher. Big Buddy Books™
is a trademark and logo of Abdo Publishing.

Printed in the United States of America, North Mankato, Minnesota.
052018
092018

Cover Photo: Chuck Place/Alamy Stock Photo.
Background Photo: zrfphoto/Getty Images.
Interior Photos: Buddy Mays/Alamy Stock Photo (p. 29); Chuck Place/Alamy Stock Photo (p. 5); David Lonstreath/
    AP Images (p. 19); Faina Gurevich/Shutterstock (p. 23); Marilyn Angel Wynn/Native Stock (pp. 9, 11, 16, 17);
    Marzolino/Shutterstock (pp. 15, 21); Paul Fearn/Alamy Stock Photo (p. 13); Kansas Historical Society (p. 30);
    Sue Ogrocki/AP Images (p. 27); WINDN/AP Images (pp. 25, 26).

Coordinating Series Editor: Tamara L. Britton
Graphic Design: Jenny Christensen, Maria Hosley

Library of Congress Control Number: 2017962676

Publisher's Cataloging-in-Publication Data

Name: Lajiness, Katie, author.
Title: Comanche / by Katie Lajiness.
Description: Minneapolis, Minnesota : Abdo Publishing, 2019. | Series: Native Americans
    set 4 | Includes online resources and index.
Identifiers: ISBN 9781532115059 (lib.bdg.) | ISBN 9781532155772 (ebook)
Subjects: LCSH: Comanche Indians--Juvenile literature. | Indians of North America--
    Juvenile literature. | Indigenous peoples--Social life and customs--Juvenile literature.
    | Cultural anthropology--Juvenile literature.
Classification: DDC 970.00497--dc23

CONTENTS

Amazing People

Hundreds of years ago, North America was mostly wild, open land. Native American tribes lived on the land. Each had its own language and **customs**.

The Comanche (kuh-MAN-chee) are one Native American tribe. Many know them for their **ceremonies** and handmade crafts. Let's learn more about these Native Americans.

Did You Know?

The name *Comanche* means "one who wants to fight with me."

4

Today, many Comanche honor their history by dancing and wearing Comanche clothes from the past.

COMANCHE TERRITORY

   The Comanche first lived in the Rocky Mountains in what is now Wyoming. In the late 1600s, they traveled on horseback through the Great Plains.

   Finally, the Comanche settled in what is now the southern United States. They controlled areas from Kansas to Texas and from New Mexico to Oklahoma. The people lived in groups called bands. Over hundreds of years, the Comanche grew from three to 12 bands.

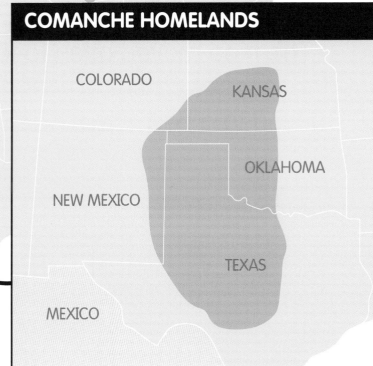

CANADA

UNITED STATES

COMANCHE HOMELANDS

COLORADO

KANSAS

NEW MEXICO

OKLAHOMA

TEXAS

MEXICO

N
W · E
S

MEXICO

HOME LIFE

The Comanche lived in teepees. These homes were made of buffalo hides and tree poles.

The tribe moved often to follow buffalo herds. The teepees could be easily taken down and moved to a new area.

Comanche set up fires in the center of the teepee for cooking and heating. An opening at the teepee's top let out the smoke.

What They Ate

These native peoples ate buffalo and deer meat. They cut the meat into strips, salted it, and laid it in the sun to dry.

The dried meat was also mixed with nuts and berries to make a trail food called pemmican. When big game was hard to find, the Comanche hunted birds and squirrels.

The Comanche rode horses while hunting for buffalo.

Daily Life

   Men and women dressed differently from one another. Men wore deerskin or elk hide pants, shirts, and moccasins. Women wore dresses and knee-high boots decorated with beads.

   Women gathered roots, berries, acorns, and onions. They raised children, cooked, and set up camp after moving to a new area.

The Comanche carried their children on cradleboards.

Men hunted bears, deer, buffalo, and elk. They also traded for corn and tobacco.

The Comanche did not waste any part of the animals they hunted. Women used animal hides for clothes and winter blankets.

Comanche began riding horses when they were four or five years old.

MADE BY HAND

The Comanche made many objects by hand. They often used natural supplies. These arts and crafts added beauty to everyday life.

Parfleche Bag
The Comanche made bags with elk hide. They decorated the bags with dyes, beadwork, and porcupine quills.

Obsidian Arrowhead

Warriors used special glass called obsidian to make arrowheads.

War Shields

Comanche war shields were made from buffalo skin. They decorated them with paint and eagle feathers.

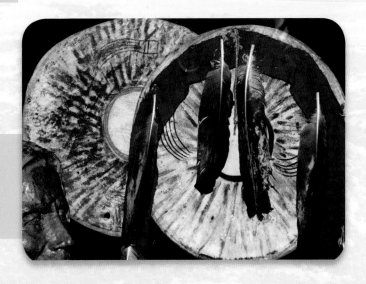

Beaded Moccasins

Women created beautiful designs by sewing beads onto leather moccasins.

Spirit Life

Comanche are deeply spiritual. They believe **medicine** men can cure sickness and guide the tribe during hard times. Some **fasted** which caused them to have **visions**. The visions helped guide their decisions.

The Comanche people believe in life after death. They honor a god called the Great Spirit.

STORYTELLERS

Like many tribes, the Comanche shared native stories. One story began long ago when all buffalo lived in a family's corral. Coyote wanted to set the buffalo free. So he changed into a puppy.

The family let the puppy live in the corral. One night, he began chasing the buffalo and they escaped. From then on, buffalo spread across North America.

Tribe members painted on their teepees to tell stories about their way of life.

FIGHTING FOR LAND

For hundreds of years, Comanche fought to keep their land. During the early 1700s, they met the Spanish settlers in what is now Colorado.

Later, the Comanche attacked New Mexico towns looking for horses. At the same time, settlers arrived in Texas. The Comanche and the Texans fought over land.

After the **Civil War**, the US government sent the Comanche to **reservations**. But the government did not provide food as it promised in **treaties**. Many Comanche went hungry.

The Comanche and the German settlers signed the Meusebach-Comanche Treaty in 1847. This was an agreement for the two groups to share land rights.

To stop the Comanche from fighting, the US Army built camps across Texas. In 1874, the Army burned Comanche villages. Nearly all Comanche had to move to **reservations** the next year. Around 1880, American hunters killed the last of the buffalo on the southern Great Plains.

Throughout most of the 1900s, the government tried to force Comanche to act like Europeans. The Comanche people would not have their own government again until the late 1900s. And they never again got control of their old lands.

In 1892, the government forced the Comanche onto small farms. The rest of the Comanche land was sold to Americans.

Back in Time

1540s
Dogs carried Comanche belongings between villages.

Late 1600s
The Comanche separated from the Shoshone tribe. Then, they left Wyoming for the Great Plains.

Early 1700s
Together with the Ute, these tribes attacked the Apache people.

Mid-1700s
The Comanche became very successful in trading and selling horses. This success made them one of the most powerful Native American groups in history.

1867

After the **Civil War**, the US Army forced the Comanche onto **reservations** under the treaty of **Medicine** Lodge.

1880

The last buffalo on the southern Great Plains were killed by hunters. This ended the Comanche way of life

1835

The tribe agreed to sign its first US **treaty**. But Texas farmers took over Comanche land.

1907

The government forced the Comanche to become Oklahoma citizens.

1922

Members of the tribe begin the Native American Church movement. In 1922, there were more than 13,300 members of the new church.

2007

The Comanche National Museum and Cultural Center opened in Oklahoma.

THE COMANCHE TODAY

The Comanche have a long, rich history. Many remember them for hunting on horseback.

Comanche roots run deep. Today, the people have held on to those special things that make them Comanche. Even though times have changed, many people carry the **traditions**, stories, and memories of the past into the present.

Did You Know?

In the early 2000s, there were about 15,000 Comanche living in the United States.

Today, Comanche children learn about their history from the older tribe members.

"My heart is filled with joy when I see you here, as the brooks fill with water when the snow melts in the spring; and I feel glad, as the ponies do when the fresh grass starts in the beginning of the year."

— Chief Ten Bears, Comanche

GLOSSARY

ceremony a formal event on a special occasion.

Civil War the war between the Northern and Southern states from 1861 to 1865.

custom a practice that has been around a long time and is common to a group or a place.

fast to go without eating food.

medicine (MEH-duh-suhn) an item used in or on the body to treat an illness, ease pain, or heal a wound.

reservation (reh-zuhr-VAY-shuhn) a piece of land set aside by the government for Native Americans to live on.

shield (SHEELD) to provide a protective cover. A shield is something that protects or hides.

tradition (truh-DIH-shuhn) a belief or a story handed down from older people to younger people.

treaty an agreement made between two or more groups.

vision something dreamed or imagined.

Online Resources

Booklinks
NONFICTION NETWORK
FREE! ONLINE NONFICTION RESOURCES

To learn more about the Comanche, visit **abdobooklinks.com**. These links are routinely monitored and updated to provide the most current information available.

INDEX